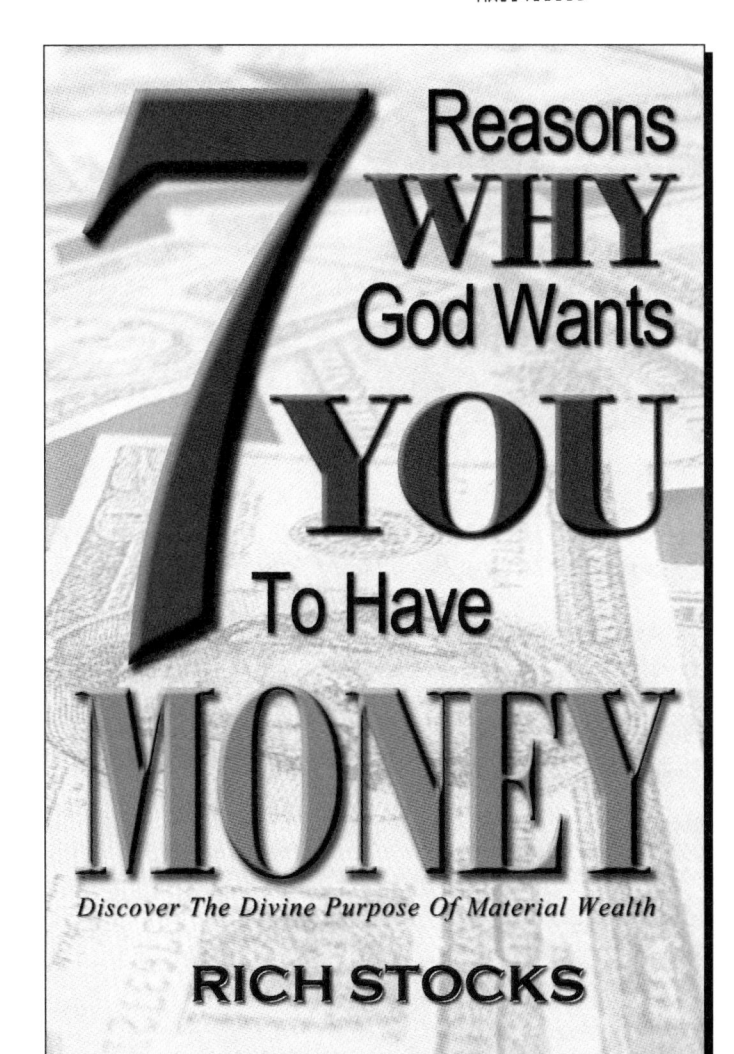

7 Reasons WHY God Wants YOU To Have MONEY

Discover The Divine Purpose Of Material Wealth

RICH STOCKS

Unless otherwise noted, all scripture references are taken from the *New King James Version* (NKJV) of *The Holy Bible*, Copyright © 1979, 1980, 1982 by Thomas Nelson, Inc. Used by permission. All rights reserved.

The following abbreviations are used for other Bible translations:

KJV– King James Version
NCV– New Century Version

Scriptures quoted from *The Holy Bible, New Century Version* ®, copyright © 1987, 1988, 1991 by Word Publishing, a division of Thomas Nelson, Inc. Used by permission.

CAPITALIZATION in scripture verses is added by the author for the purposes of emphasis only.

7 Reasons WHY God Wants YOU To Have Money
Discover the Divine Purpose of Material Wealth

Published and Copyright ©2005 by Rich Stocks Ministries, Inc.
Tulsa, Oklahoma

Cover design, editing, and typesetting by James Rizzuti

Library of Congress Cataloging-in-Publication Data

Stocks, Rich
7 Reasons WHY God Wants YOU To Have Money
Discover the Divine Purpose of Material Wealth

ISBN 0-9769253-0-3
1. Money
2. Gospel of Jesus Christ
3. Faith

All rights reserved. No portion of this book may be reproduced in any form without the written permission of the publisher.

Printed in the United States of America

A Special Thanks

...to the following friends and partners
who helped turn this dream into a reality.

Brian Aikey
Joshua Halcomb
Daniel and Caroline Jensen
Dale and Betty Prater
Margie Ramsey
Verl and Cathy Richmond
James and Leslie Rizzuti
Loren and Wanda Schoeneman
Garlan and Gail Summers
Vern and Mary Talbert
Carl and Joyce Tesreau
James Vance

May all of YOUR dreams be fulfilled!
Rich Stocks

About The Author

Rich Stocks is an experienced Bible teacher and successful businessman.

He began ministering at the age of nineteen, speaking for churches, youth functions, correctional facilities, and wherever there was an open door. After graduation from high school, he also served a summer on the mission field in Mexico. In addition, Rich has filled various positions as Youth Minister, Associate Pastor, Interim Pastor, and Senior Pastor, and has hosted his own daily radio broadcast. Rich has also has made television appearances on TBN, (Trinity Broadcasting Network's) *"Doctor To Doctor"* program.

After several years of full-time ministry, Rich sensed a leading to attend *Rhema Bible Training Center* in Broken Arrow, Oklahoma, where he and his wife Dee graduated in 2001.

Both Rich and Dee also have earned a B.A. degree in Theology from *Golden Grain Bible College and Seminary* in Ventura, California.

In 1997, Rich started in the nutrition business with just six dollars and helped develop it into a multi-million dollar international business within five years. Through his business, Rich and his family enjoyed the opportunity of living in Australia for a year.

Dee Stocks is an anointed Psalmist, Songwriter, and Worship Leader. She has served as a Worship Leader in various churches for more than twelve years, and has traveled and ministered both in the Word and in song.

Together, Rich and Dee have a vision to help encourage, equip, and empower believers, ministers, and businessmen to fulfill their God-given purpose and potential.

Rich and Dee have four children and currently live in Tulsa, Oklahoma.

Contents

    A Special Thanks...3

    About the Author...4

1. The Importance of Understanding "Why"..............................7

2. God Knows 13

3. The Priority of Providing 21

4. Keeping Your Promises 29

5. The Father's Love 41

6. Enjoying the Fruit of Your Labor..49

7. Life's Greatest Blessing 57

8. Kingdom Building...67

9. How Much Money Does God Want Me to Have? 77

10. The Father's Pleasure 85

    Closing Thoughts and Prayer 91

Chapter 1
The Importance of Understanding "Why"

God wants you to have money. In the next few chapters, you are going to find out why. You are about to discover the Divine purpose of material wealth! In this book, we will look at *seven specific reasons* why God wants you to have money, each of which is clearly presented in the Word of God.

There are probably more than seven reasons, but these seven are undeniable, and they will give you a solid foundation on which you can build. The purpose of this book is not to try to convince you that God wants you to have money, but rather to help you understand the reasons *why*.

Knowledge And Understanding
God's ministers are supposed to feed His people with

two types of spiritual food. Let's look at this in Scripture.

> **"And I will give you pastors according to mine heart, which shall feed you with KNOWLEDGE and UNDERSTANDING."**
> **(Jeremiah 3:15, KJV)**

Notice God says that the desire of His heart is that we be fed, not just with knowledge, but with both *"KNOWLEDGE AND UNDERSTANDING."* So what's the difference?

Knowledge is an accumulation of facts and information that generally answers questions like "What?" "When?" or "Where?" Understanding provides a deeper knowledge that goes beyond the facts, and helps answer questions like "How?" and "Why?" Why is this distinction so important? Understanding the "How?" and "Why?" of anything strengthens beliefs, and makes believing easier.

If you understand how something works, and why it works, you will have a much stronger foundation for believing that it does indeed work.

If I can show you seven reasons "Why" God wants you to have money, then you will probably never again question the fact that God does want you to have material wealth. So, both KNOWLEDGE and UNDERSTANDING are essential for faith. That is why faith comes by hearing God's Word.

When God's ministers feed us with knowledge and understanding from the Word of God, our faith increases. Our ability to believe is directly related to our knowledge and understanding.

Our faith is limited to our level of knowledge and understanding. We could say it like this: *The greater knowledge and understanding you have of any subject, the stronger your beliefs will be.* Not only that, but answering the question "Why?" often can help with understanding the true purpose of something.

Money – Good or Evil?
The Bible declares that everything God made is good and has a purpose.

> **"Then God saw EVERYTHING THAT HE HAD MADE, and indeed it was very good..."**
> **(Genesis 1:31)**

Who made money? Well, if we are talking about paper money, of course man printed it. But who really made money? Who created the gold, the silver, and the precious resources of the Earth that give the printed paper money its value?

If you are a Bible believer, you know for sure that God created everything, including material wealth like gold and silver. Not only do we know that He created it, but we also know that God looked at everything He made, including the valuable resources we use to buy and sell, and He said, "It is good."

So if everything God made is good, then money must be good, because God made it. Don't ever let yourself be tricked into believing that there is anything evil about money. I have heard well-meaning believers and even preachers say that money is the root of all evil. Nothing could be further from the truth. That is not what the Bible says.

> **"For the LOVE OF MONEY is the root of all evil..."**
> **(1 Timothy 6:10, KJV)**

It is not money that is evil, but the love of it that is evil. It is very important that you understand this. How could God say that something He created is good, but then tell us that loving it is the root of all evil? This is a great question, and will lead us to the very essence of what this book is about.

God made money, and money is good, but loving it is bad. Why? Because the person who loves money does not understand why God wants him to have it.

The Divine Purpose
In reading the account of creation in the book of Genesis, it is clear to me that the world is not the result of an experiment. It is a pre-determined and detailed masterpiece by a Master Designer. God put a lot of thought and planning into His creation.

Therefore, everything that God made must have a purpose. I like to call this *"The Divine Purpose."* The Divine purpose of something is the purpose for which

God intended it. If all of God's creation has a "Why?" or a reason for existence, then there must be a Divine purpose for material riches.

It is very important that we understand the Divine purpose of wealth. Without a clear understanding of the purpose of something, it is difficult, perhaps impossible, to receive the full benefit for which it was created.

In addition, when purposes become perverted or distorted, even good things like intelligence, physical strength, influence, authority, electricity, and even money can become dangerous. A lack of understanding of the purpose of anything leads to misuse, abuse, and error. Throughout history, people have misused their power, their influence, their wealth, and even the Scriptures. The results of this are devastating.

There is another important reason to learn why God wants you to have money. Through my experience in business, I have learned that all business people need a "Why?" What does this mean?

It's not only important to have written goals and to know what you want, but it is perhaps even more important to know *why* you want to achieve those goals. Your "Why?" is your true motivation. It's what keeps you going and enables you to persevere, even through the tough times, until you reach your goals.

Simply put, without a strong "Why?" a person will rarely achieve or obtain the things he desires. If you don't know why you really want something, it's very unlikely that you will ever have it, and even if you did, it probably wouldn't bring you much long-term joy or satisfaction.

However, if your "Why?" is strong enough, and clearly defined, you are more likely to find the motivation necessary to do whatever it takes to reach your goals.

Having a strong "Why?" will also help you find more contentment and a much deeper sense of fulfillment once your goals have been achieved. Many Christians would like to have more money. If you don't believe it, just ask a few of them. In fact, chances are you won't even have to ask. Hang around believers long enough and they will let you know. These same people may even believe that it's God's will for them to have more money. But if you asked them "Why?" they might struggle to come up with a legitimate answer.

I am absolutely convinced that the greatest hindrance to financial prosperity in the Body of Christ is a lack of knowledge and understanding of the Divine purpose for which material riches were created.

Once you find out the real reasons why God wants you to have money, they will empower your faith, help diminish your doubts, and hopefully will motivate you to do all that is necessary to begin to increase financially. So let's find out "Why" God wants you to have money!

Chapter 2
God Knows

The first reason why God wants you to have money is the most basic. It is simply a matter of common sense. The answer is found in Matthew, chapter six.

> "Therefore do not worry, saying, 'What shall we eat?' or 'What shall we drink?' or 'What shall we wear?' For after all these things the Gentiles seek. For your heavenly Father knows that you NEED ALL THESE THINGS."
> **(Matthew 6:31-32)**

This scripture gives us a very sound reason why God wants us to have money, and that is because He knows that we need it to survive. God knows that we need all of these material things like food, water, clothing, and shelter to survive. He knows that money is the means of exchange most commonly used to obtain all of these things. God wants you to have money because He knows that it is an absolute necessity. What a simple concept.

God made a physical man, put him in a material world, created a system of exchange called buying and selling, and He wants you to have money because it is essential for your survival. So, the first and most basic reason why God wants you to have money is because you must have it to survive.

You might say, "Well I know someone who is surviving without money." No, you don't. You don't know one person who is surviving without money. It just isn't possible.

You may know someone who is surviving without any of their *own* money, but I can assure you that they are surviving off of *someone's* money.

Pause with me for a moment, and try to think of something that you can do in this world that doesn't require money. I would be curious to see your list after you think about it for a while. I can't think of anything that can be done without money. It takes money to be born; it takes money to live, and it even takes money to die.

Before you were ever born, you were costing someone money. Your parents had to prepare for your birth. The food your mother was consuming was supporting your survival. There was a pregnancy test, then medical care, transportation to and from the doctor, and so on. Then it cost money to bring you into the world. Most of us were born in a hospital with the help of medical professionals. All of this costs money.

Once you were born, the budget really increased. Then there was infant formula, diapers, special supplies to care for you, toys to play with, and the list goes on.

If you have children, then you know exactly what I'm talking about. All I have to say is, "Just wait until they become teenagers!" I currently have three teenagers and they still like toys. The challenge is that the toys just keep getting bigger and more expensive!

I Wasn't Interested
I remember when I was nineteen years old, during my first year of college. I recently had become excited about God, and about the things I was learning from the Word of God. During this time a very popular teaching in the church was the "prosperity message." Men and women of God were boldly declaring that God wanted His people to have plenty of money.

I have to be honest with you, of all the things I was learning from the Bible, this message of prosperity was of little or no interest to me.

Every time someone started teaching about God's plan for financial increase, I just sat there hoping they would move on to something more "spiritual."

Why wasn't I interested in this vital subject?

Well, I was still a teenager; I had no wife, no children, no debts, and very few financial responsibilities. I had a part-time job, and my parents had given me a small savings account when I graduated from high school. I also had a scholarship to attend college for free, so it was easy for me to survive. It wasn't that I didn't believe in prosperity, I just wasn't interested in hearing about it.

Here is a key that we discussed in the last chapter. I saw no purpose for learning about prosperity because I did not understand "Why" God wanted me to have money.

Eventually I got married, and my interests suddenly changed. Let me tell you, I quickly decided that I would take a second look at this "prosperity message." Read the first few chapters in the book of Genesis, and you will see that God gave man a job BEFORE He gave him a wife.

Adam's job was to work in the garden and to guard it. Guys, this is called a CLUE! Ladies, it's called a CLUE! I have two daughters, and when they were very young I gave them a list of requirements that must be met by any guy who comes under consideration as a potential husband.

Then, several years later, I added one more requirement to the list. **HE MUST HAVE A GOOD JOB!** It sounds a little humorous, but it is also very serious. Most importantly, it is very scriptural, as you will see in the next chapter. Guys, please hear me. It is CRUCIAL that you get a good job BEFORE you get a wife. Just this one small piece of advice can save you years of unnecessary misery.

We are still talking about why God wants you to have money. You need it to survive. Money is not an option; it's not a luxury; it is a necessity.

A couple of years after getting married, my wife and I had our first child. Now this single young man, who had no interest in money, had two more people whose survival depended on him and the money he was called to provide.

By this time I was ready to take a much closer look at the *"prosperity message."* Then we had another child, another, and another. HELP! Now I was eagerly, (more like desperately) devouring every book, every tape, and every verse I could find on the subject of money.

So in just a few short years, I went from having no interest in prosperity, to becoming a full-fledged prosperity preacher. Why? What caused the change? The change occurred as I experienced first hand the revelation of why God wanted me to have money. God wants us to have money because we need money to survive.

Can You Afford To Die?
Let's go back to the example I mentioned earlier in this chapter. I said that we need money before we are born, we need money to be born, we need money to survive after we are born, and we need money to die.

Perhaps you're thinking, "I don't need money to die. Once I'm gone, my financial responsibilities and worries will be over." Really? What an irresponsible attitude.

I have actually heard people say, "I'm not leaving any money for my kids to fight over. After I'm gone, it's their problem, not mine." So who's going to pay for you to die? "Pay for me to die?" Yes, who is going to pay for your death, your funeral, your casket, and your burial plot?

In fact, let's take it a step further. Not only does it take money to be born, to live, and to die; it also costs money AFTER you die.

"After I'm gone?" Yes. Do you realize that even after you are dead and gone, someone will have to pay the debts that you leave behind? Someone will have to take care of your financial obligations.

I have known people who have lost houses, property, and other types of inheritance, because they had to take care of the financial obligations of someone who was dead and gone. Make a note of this fact. Just because you die, it does not mean that your financial obligations disappear. Someone will have to pay them, and for you or I not to be concerned about it is a total disregard of our responsibilities.

You can leave behind a financial BLESSING, or a financial CURSE for an inheritance. Even if you don't have one living relative when you pass away, someone will have to pay for your death.

Maybe you think the government will pay for it. Who is the government, and where does the government get money? It comes out of our pockets. The government is funded by individuals like you and me. I hope I have driven home the reality of the first and most basic reason why God wants you to have money. Let's review.

- **It takes money before we are born.**
- **It takes money to be born.**
- **It takes money to live.**
- **It takes money to die.**
- **It takes money after we die.**

Friend, you can't do ANYTHING without money. God wants you to have money because He knows that it is absolutely necessary for your survival in this world. Now, let's find out the second reason why God wants you to have money.

Chapter 3
The Priority of Providing

In this chapter I will share with you the second reason why God wants you to have money. I briefly touched on this concept in the previous chapter, but let's examine it more thoroughly. Once again we will look in the Word of God to find our answer.

> **"But if anyone does not PROVIDE FOR HIS OWN, and especially for THOSE OF HIS HOUSEHOLD, he has denied the faith and is worse than an unbeliever."**
> **(1 Timothy 5:8)**

The second reason why God wants you to have money is to provide for your family. *The Amplified Bible* says that a believer who does not provide for his family is worse than an unbeliever who does. Imagine that.

Friend, it's time that we stop trying to be so spiritual that we overlook the obvious. Evidently, providing for man's material needs is very high on God's priority list.

Providing for the family is primarily the responsibility of the man of the house, but unfortunately it could become the responsibility of the woman of the house as well. I say unfortunately, because I am convinced that a woman should only provide money in the house if she wants to, not because she has to.

So ladies, I'm not being chauvinistic. If you enjoy working and providing, that is fine. It's between you, your family, and the Lord. In no way am I suggesting that a woman is less qualified, or is not capable of providing. But, it is sad to me that so many women have been thrust into a situation where they have no choice but to work outside of the home, just so the family can get by.

The Scripture we looked at seems to indicate that it is the man's responsibility to provide. Notice the words "he" and "his."

> **"But if anyone does not provide for HIS own, and especially for those of HIS household, HE has denied the faith and is worse than an unbeliever."**
> **(1 Timothy 5:8)**

I looked up this scripture in several translations, and each one implied that the person called to provide is the man of the house. However, ladies, maybe you have found yourself in a situation where the man is gone or has chosen not to fulfill his obligation to provide. In this case you may be forced to become the provider.

Notice the strong language that is used in this verse. God said that providing for your family is so important, that if you don't provide, you are *"WORSE THAN AN UNBELIEVER!"* He did not say you were equal to an unbeliever, he said you were *"WORSE THAN"* an unbeliever.

Folks, according to this verse, money is a very serious matter. I'm not sure many believers have grasped the urgency, or the value that the scripture places on this subject of money. I know for sure, that for years, I did not.

I mentioned in the last chapter that, as a young single college student, I didn't have a clue regarding the importance or value of money. But when I married and had children, that all changed. I mean it changed quickly!

Now there was infant formula, diapers, and much more. As my children have become teenagers, our family requires even more money. A lot more! I wish someone had taught me these principles before I got married and started a family. They could have saved me a lot of unnecessary suffering.

I'm actually almost ashamed to admit how ignorant I really was and how poorly I provided during those early years of marriage.

This verse describes my life back then quite well:

> **"My people are destroyed for LACK OF KNOWLEDGE..."**
> **(Hosea 4:6)**

My lack of knowledge concerning the importance of money almost destroyed me and my family. During those early years, I was very confused. I knew that I was called to the ministry. I also knew that God's best was that I earn my living through the ministry. However, what I didn't understand was just how important providing for my family was in the eyes of God. I have yet to find the verse that says if we drag our feet in fulfilling our ministry that we are worse than an unbeliever, but God does say this to the man who does not provide financially for his family.

Don't misunderstand me. It is essential that we fulfill whatever God has called us to do. But, you must realize that one of your primary callings is to provide for your family. This is a basic obligation for every man on this planet. I believe in this so strongly that I plan to write an entire book emphasizing the fact that our job is more important than our ministry.

It appears that even Jesus had to be faithful in his job *before* He entered the ministry. What was Jesus doing, and how was he surviving all those years, before he started preaching? If we cannot handle our own business, how can we possibly expect to handle the Father's business? If we cannot be faithful in providing material things for our own family, how can we possibly be trusted as ministers to provide the spiritual things of God to those outside of our family?

Who Is Our Family?
If we are to provide for our family, the next question is, "Who is included in this group?" Who is our family? Are you supposed to provide for all of your in-laws, your aunts, uncles, nieces, nephews, cousins, and second cousins?

I think that the scripture we read earlier in 1 Timothy 5:8 gives us some insight. Notice it said, *"...especially for those of his own household."*

It appears that our primary financial responsibility is to our immediate family members who are living in the same house with us. This would certainly include your wife and children, and in some cases could include others who have become part of your household.

The Bible also talks about providing for widows who are older and not likely to re-marry. You might want to read the entire passage found in 1 Timothy 5:8-16. Let's look at just one verse from that passage.

> **"Let me remind you again that a widow's relatives must take care of her, and not leave this to the church to do. Then the church can spend its money for the care of widows who are all alone and have nowhere else to turn."**
> **(1 Timothy 5:16, The Living Bible)**

The Word of God also speaks about honoring our parents. One way that we can honor our parents is by helping to take care of them.

I am convinced that if parents should ever find themselves in a time of life where they cannot provide for themselves, the children are the ones who should take care of them. It's sort of amazing that when we are children, God expects our parents to take care of us, and then years later, if necessary, we are expected to take care of them.

So who is our family that we have an obligation to provide for? Those living in the same house with us, parents who can no longer provide for themselves, and older widows who are close relatives. Let's look at another verse that talks about providing financially for our family.

> **"A good man leaves an inheritance to his CHILDREN'S CHILDREN, But the wealth of the sinner is stored up for the righteous."**
> **(Proverbs 13:22)**

Some would argue that this verse is talking about something other than a material inheritance. The inheritance you leave behind doesn't have to be limited to material wealth, but this is obviously the subject referred to in this verse.

I always like to take the most literal interpretation of scripture first. Since the second half of the verse mentions *"the wealth of the sinner,"* I know for sure that this scripture is referring to money. A sinner certainly cannot leave behind a "spiritual" inheritance, because he is spiritually bankrupt.

So, in addition to providing for our own children, we should also be looking down the road and making plans to bless our grandchildren. I don't believe that this verse means that you should leave all of your wealth for your grandchildren, and not leave any for your children. That sure could create some ill feelings toward you after you're gone.

No, I'm convinced that this means that God wants you to be so blessed that you not only leave behind enough to bless your children, but it's enough to bless your grandchildren as well. How many believers do you know who are in a financial position to fulfill this verse? As I mentioned in the last chapter, some people not only fail to leave behind a financial blessing, they actually leave behind a financial curse of unpaid debts.

Money – Spiritual, or Non-Spiritual?
I just can't seem to let go of this thought that we must be very careful how we categorize "spiritual" or "non-spiritual" issues. We live in a physical world, and our physical needs are so important to God that He says neglecting to provide for these basic needs makes us worse than someone who does not even believe the Gospel.

Your spirit, and even God's Spirit, (if you are a Christian) lives in your physical body. That physical body will always have physical needs, and we have clearly established the fact that money is the tool most commonly used to provide for those physical needs. So ask yourself this question: How important is money in the eyes of God? The answer to that question is so stunning that it shook me to the core of my being.

IF I DO NOT PROVIDE FOR MY FAMILY, I AM WORSE THAN AN UNBELIEVER!

This one verse that we have been looking at in this chapter overturned my theological applecart and caused me to rethink and re-define what true spirituality really is.

Friend, the only conclusion I can come to is that money must be far more "spiritual" than most believers seem to realize. Perhaps this is why Jesus not only preached to the multitudes, he also fed them. Jesus performed what I call financial miracles or miracles of provision. He multiplied physical food, (fish and bread) and fed the thousands of followers who had come to hear his message.

Money is spiritual, because if your physical needs don't get met, you won't be around long to do very many spiritual things.

So far we have discovered two very important reasons why God wants you to have money. First, God wants you to have money because He knows that you need it to survive, and secondly, He wants you to have money to provide for your family. Now let's move on, and find the third reason why God wants you to have money.

Chapter 4
Keeping Your Promises

There are at least seven reasons why God wants you to have money. So far we have discussed two of them. First, we learned that God wants you to have money to survive, and then we saw that God wants you to have money to provide for your family. Now let's look at a third reason why God wants you to have money.

"The wicked borrows and does not repay..."
(Psalm 37:21)

The third reason why God wants you to have money is so you can pay your debts. God wants you to fulfill your financial obligations. In fact, this scripture says that failure to pay debts is a characteristic of a wicked person. I would like to rename *"Paying Your Debts"* as

"Keeping Your Promises," because that is exactly what debts are. A debt is a promise to pay a certain amount of money by a certain time. Notice what the Word of God says about keeping promises:

> **"If a man makes a vow to the LORD, or swears an oath to bind himself by some agreement, he shall not break his word; he shall do according to all that proceeds out of his mouth."**
> **(Numbers 30:2)**

> **"It is better not to promise anything than to promise something and not do it. Don't let your words cause you to sin..."**
> **(Ecclesiastes 5:5-6, NCV)**

God takes the subject of keeping promises very seriously. This verse indicates that breaking a promise is sin. So we could say it like this: *Neglecting to pay your debts, (not keeping your financial promises) is sin.* Perhaps this rewording will help us take the matter more seriously.

If there is anyone in the world who should be diligent in the area of keeping financial promises, it should be the child of God. However, I am sad to report that, often, this is not the case.

The Mechanic Story
I am reminded of an auto mechanic who was a pretty good friend of mine. He had a very reputable business, and was a strong believer with high integrity. Back in

those days I drove old beat-up cars, so I got to see him quite often.

One day, as he was working on my car, a fellow believer pulled into the driveway of this man's business. My friend said with despair in his voice, "Oh, No!" I knew that the man who had just arrived was a good Christian brother, so I asked my friend what was wrong.

He said, "I hate to see Christians pulling in my driveway." I couldn't believe my ears, so in amazement I asked him why.

He said, "I never have a problem getting a sinner to pay a bill. I never have a sinner ask me for credit, or if they can pay me later. But almost every Christian who does business with me, either does not want to pay, wants to pay me later, or expects me to charge them less than I charge everybody else."

I was beginning to see the light of what Jesus meant in the following scripture:

> **"...for the children of this world are in their generation wiser than the children of light."**
> **(Luke 16:8, KJV)**

What is this verse referring to? If you read the entire passage, beginning with the first verse of this chapter, you will see that the story is about an unjust employee's practical method in dealing with money. So let's rephrase what Jesus said in modern language. *"Sinners are generally smarter in dealing with practical matters, like money, than believers are."*

Let me add an additional note to the mechanic story. My friend had a huge sign hanging in his shop that read,

"NO CREDIT! DON'T ASK! IN GOD I TRUST, ALL OTHERS PAY CASH!"

I had seen that sign many times, and laughed every time I saw it. It was a very humorous, but also a very straightforward way to get a message across loud and clear. Because the message was so easy to understand, I never even considered asking my friend if I could pay him later, or if he could reduce my bill, even though I was struggling financially in a big way.

So you can imagine how shocked I was to hear that the majority of Christians that he did business with asked for credit, especially with this big bold sign hanging right in their face. I just couldn't believe it.

I suppose that back then I was a bit naïve. I just assumed that believers had more integrity and character than sinners did. In the years to come, I began to see that this is not necessarily the case.

Far too many Christians seem to think they are exempt from practical responsibilities like paying debts, when in fact, we ought to be the most responsible group in the world.

My Encounter With An Irresponsible Believer

I could tell you story after story that illustrates this fact. I do have to tell you one more. I managed a successful business, and decided to move my family to Australia for a year to start the business there.

We had tried for some time to sell our home, but nothing was happening. We eventually decided to lease the house for a year and take off. We interviewed a few prospective tenants, and decided on a particular lady, primarily because she seemed to be a sincere believer, and she was.

However, she suffered from this same irresponsible attitude that is common in the Body of Christ. What a nightmare it turned out to be! The lady was very polite, and paid her rent on time almost every month, up until near the end of the lease.

A couple of months before the lease expired, and before our return to the United States, I began to make fairly frequent contact with her, to make sure she understood that we would be back soon. I strongly encouraged her not to wait until the last minute to find another place to live. I began to get uneasy. It didn't seem to me that she was making an effort to find another home, even though she had known for a year when we would return.

Eventually I realized that she wasn't planning to move out of our house. She even made comments like, "I believe that God wants me to have this house." Well, I was on the other side of the world, and didn't know quite how to handle it. Let me assure you, I thought of several plans, some of which were quite severe. I'm sure that you have never had thoughts like that.

To make a long story short, we arrived back in the United States with no place to live. It was Christmas time, and we actually spent Christmas that year in a hotel.

After making every attempt to get her to move, we eventually went through the legal system. I even found her another house to move into, but she never lifted a finger to move. It took a month to get her out of our house.

The deputy sheriff paid her a visit and told her that he would be back in forty-eight hours to physically move her out, and to change the locks on the doors. Sure enough, I arrived with the deputy forty-eight hours later, and we moved her, and her family, out of the house. She had not packed anything, not one stitch of clothing, not one dish, not a thing. She left all of her furniture, electronic equipment, everything.

I'm still dumfounded by this lady's irresponsible attitude. At one point I asked her if she had even made an honest effort to try to find another home, and she said "No." She insisted that God wanted her to have our house, so she never even made an attempt to find another place to live.

She didn't really care that I had a family, that we were back from a year of living overseas, and that we just wanted to relax and enjoy Christmas in our own home. I just couldn't seem to get her to understand that this was not her house, that she had no right to stay there past the agreed upon date, and that she had no grounds to expect God to defend her cause.

I tried to reason with her, and even pointed out the errors of her beliefs and actions in light of scripture, but she just wouldn't listen. Why? Even though she was a sincere believer, she was sincerely mixed up.

What she failed to understand was that her "spirituality" did not make her exempt from fulfilling her practical obligations. She didn't keep her promise to me to be out of the house by a certain date, and no matter how she tried to justify it, it was wrong.

Setting The Standard
As believers, we should be the ones who set the Godly example for the rest of the world to follow. Isn't that what Jesus meant when he said that we are the salt of the Earth and the light of the world? We talk about "witnessing," but what about *being* a good witness?

Your greatest witness is the life you live before your fellow man. If you want people to listen to you when you tell them about Jesus, then show them the true nature and character of Jesus by paying your bills on time. I believe that God wants us to be "squeaky-clean" when it comes to keeping our promises.

Let's make sure that we don't give the world a legitimate reason to criticize us. I realize that Jesus was perfect, and He was still criticized and persecuted. But, a lot of what we call "persecution" has nothing to do with being persecuted for our Christianity, but for our lack of Christian ethics and values.

Not only should we pay our debts, but we should pay them on time. Remember, a debt is an agreement, (a promise) to pay a certain amount by a certain time. Here is a scripture that reinforces this concept:

> **"Do not withhold good from those TO WHOM IT IS DUE, When it is in the power of your hand to do so. Do not say to your neighbor, 'Go, and come back, And TOMORROW I will give it,' When you have it with you."**
> **(Proverbs 3:27-28)**

This verse may have more than one application, but the words *"TO WHOM IT IS DUE"* says to me that this would definitely apply to paying the people we owe.

The message is simple. Pay your debts on time! Don't ever make someone wait for a payment, unless it is absolutely impossible for you to pay it.

What Would Jesus Do?
Don't you just love the acronym, "WWJD – What Would Jesus Do?" Think about it. What would Jesus do if He had debts? He would pay them on time! Jesus was even asked about paying taxes. Notice what He said:

> "....Render therefore to Caesar the things that are Caesar's, and to God the things that are God's."
> (Matthew 22:21)

Here is yet another verse that speaks of the importance of fulfilling our financial obligations.

> "This is also why you pay taxes. Rulers are working for God and give their time to their work. Pay everyone, then, what you owe. If you owe any kind of tax, pay it. Show respect and honor to them all."
> (Romans 13:6-7, NCV)

I want to take this thought a step further. God may even require you to pay a bill that you don't really owe, just for the sake of keeping a good name and a good reputation for yourself, and for the Kingdom of God. Here is a perfect example.

> "When they had come to Capernaum, those who received the temple tax came to Peter and said, 'Does your Teacher not pay the temple tax?' He said, 'Yes.' And when he had come into the house, Jesus anticipated him, saying, 'What do you think, Simon? From whom do the kings of the earth take customs or taxes, from their sons or from strangers?' Peter said to Him, 'From strangers.' Jesus said to him, 'Then the sons are free. Nevertheless, lest we offend them, go to the sea, cast in a

> **hook, and take the fish that comes up first. And when you have opened its mouth, you will find a piece of money; take that and give it to them for Me and you.'"**
> **(Matthew 17:24-27)**

I have heard different teachings on this passage, but the one thing that is clear to me is that Jesus had no intention of paying this temple tax. He plainly says that *"the sons are free,"* indicating that neither he, nor Peter, owed the money. It was not a legitimate debt. But notice that it was so important to Jesus to keep a good name, and a good reputation, and to keep from offending the other religious leaders, that He paid the temple tax anyway. This is another powerful example of the importance God places on us having a good reputation regarding money matters.

No Condemnation

Now is a good time for me to say this. In no way is it my intention to make anyone feel guilty or condemned. I realize that sometimes we get ourselves into such a financial bind that we just cannot pay our bills on time. Trust me, I know. I've been there.

In fact, I went through a period of years where I was seldom able to pay anything on time. People think I'm just kidding when I tell them, *"I WAS SO BROKE I COULDN'T EVEN PAY ATTENTION!"*

I felt like the Momma Duck, when she saw all her baby ducks. *"NOTHING BUT BILLS...BILLS...BILLS!"* How did it happen? It was easy: a few kids, a few credit cards, and a few bad decisions, and I was in a mess. After all these years, the enemy still tries to make me feel guilty over my past financial failures. I have to treat it like I would any other sin. I missed it; I repented; I have been forgiven, and I am moving on.

Perhaps you are at a time in your life when you are really struggling financially. I can say with all sincerity that I know how you feel. At times the pressure may seem unbearable. I have known people who have taken their own lives because of financial pressures.

My prayer for you right now is that the Holy Spirit of God will show you the steps to take that will lead you out of the difficulty that you're in.

I also pray that God will move supernaturally on your behalf, just like He did when Peter was concerned about paying the temple tax. I am asking God to give you a financial miracle that will help you get started on the road to financial recovery.

Friend, God wants you to keep your promises. God wants you to have money so you can fulfill your financial obligations, be a good witness, and avoid bringing a reproach upon the name of Christ and Christianity.

Chapter 5
The Father's Love

So far I've given you three solid reasons why God wants you to have money.

1. **God knows that you need money to survive.**

2. **God wants you to provide for your family. It is a high priority.**

3. **God wants you to keep your promises by paying your debts on time.**

Before I give you the fourth reason why God wants you to have money, we need to pause and cover another very important subject. Initially, I planned to include these thoughts at the end of the previous chapter, but I realized that understanding this subject is so important that I needed to devote an entire chapter to it.

I will be the first to admit that money is not the most important thing in your life. However, I do agree with a humorous comment that I heard a motivational speaker say. He said,

"MONEY MAY NOT BE EVERYTHING, BUT IT RANKS RIGHT UP THERE WITH OXYGEN!"

What a concept! I agree wholeheartedly. The Bible does tell us what the most important thing in our life should be.

"Wisdom is the most important thing;…"
(Proverbs 4:7, NCV)

I won't say a lot about this right now, but I am currently working on another book about wisdom. One thing I will say is that wisdom is the ability to make right decisions. I am convinced that this is why there is a wisdom-money connection in the Bible. Apart from Jesus, Solomon was the wisest man who ever lived, and as a direct result of his wisdom he was also the *wealthiest* man who ever lived.

"Wait a minute; I thought that God gave Solomon all that wealth."

Yes He did, but again let's ask "How?" and "Why?" I am convinced that Solomon's wisdom, (his ability to make right decisions) is what enabled him to receive and multiply the wealth that God had promised him. Solomon's decision-making ability made it easy for God to get the wealth to him, and I'm sure made it easier for him to take what God gave him and cause it to increase.

I don't believe that Solomon woke up one morning, walked outside, and saw heaps of gold and silver all over his yard. I'm certainly not saying that it's impossible, but it probably didn't happen that way. This next passage indicates that wisdom is a key to riches:

> **"Happy is the man who finds wisdom …Length of days is in her right hand, In her left hand RICHES and honor."**
> **(Proverbs 3:13, 16)**

Suppose that you were to receive a major financial breakthrough. If you didn't exercise wisdom by making right decisions, it would all just disappear and soon you would find yourself back in the same bind that you were in before God gave you the miracle.

The point I'm trying to make is that, whatever financial state you are in right now, it is directly connected to the level of wisdom you are exercising in making your decisions. In other words, your decisions, (whether good or bad) have created your financial world. I like what I heard a very seasoned man of God say:

"YOU MAKE DECISIONS, THEN YOUR DECISIONS MAKE YOU!"

Can you see the need to devote an entire book to this subject? So wherever you are financially today, it's a result of decisions you have made.

I have already told you that I went through a period of extreme financial lack and pressure. It lasted for years. As I look back now, I can see that I didn't have to suffer one day. All of my financial woes were a direct result of poor decisions that I made. My severe lack of wisdom produced a severe lack of wealth in my life.

WISDOM AND WEALTH HAVE AN INSEPARABLE CONNECTION.

I needed to say all of that to say this: Some people would say, "Why should God prosper someone who is in a bad way because of their own bad decisions? Yes, I believe that God wants me to have money to survive, to provide for my family, and to pay my bills, but because of my bad decisions I never seem to have enough. So maybe God just wants to let me suffer for a while, so I can learn to make right decisions concerning money."

I know that some people will read this book, especially the section on paying debts, and they will present this argument. "God didn't sign for the debt, so He's not obligated to help pay it. The man or woman borrowed the money, so they shouldn't expect God to help them pay it back."

I have even heard preachers make these types of remarks. All I can say is that the person who thinks this way does not understand the nature of his Heavenly Father. God loves you unconditionally, and if you are born again, you are His child.

If your child had a debt that he or she couldn't pay, and you had the ability to help them, what would you do?

> **"If you then, being evil, know how to give good gifts to your children, HOW MUCH MORE will your Father who is in heaven give good things to those who ask Him!"**
> **(Matthew 7:11)**

You might say, "Yes, but what if the debt is a direct result of a foolish decision?"

This verse doesn't say that God only gives to those who never make a bad decision. So God's giving must be based on something other than our merit.

Let me ask you a question: Do you honestly believe that God only wants to help those who deserve it? If this were true then none of us would ever have a chance to be saved and receive eternal life.

We are saved by God's grace, which is His unmerited favor. Our part is simply to accept His grace by faith.

Most believers accept this truth with regard to their salvation, but many seem to struggle in applying this same principle to all the other areas of their lives. Just substitute whatever it is you need for the word "saved" in the following verse, and it will be a great help to you.

> "For by grace you have been saved through faith, and that not of yourselves; it is the gift of God."
>
> **(Ephesians 2:8)**

I have heard many believers say, *"The good Lord helps those who help themselves."* This is true, but part two should say, *"And He also helps those who CANNOT help themselves."* We could even add a third part to this statement. *"God even helps those who do not deserve His help."*

> "...For He is kind to the unthankful and evil."
>
> **(Luke 6:35)**

The Prodigal Son

Anyone who makes comments about God not being obligated to help us pay our debts, simply does not understand the Father's love. In Luke, chapter fifteen, we find one of the most beautiful examples of this in the whole Bible. It's the story of *"The Prodigal Son."*

The son took the inheritance that His father had given him and wasted all of it on parties and prostitutes. He hit such a financial low that he ended up in a pigpen eating with the pigs. It doesn't get much worse than that, does it?

One day the son decided that he'd had enough. He decided to go back home to his father's house. Look what happened!

THE FATHER'S LOVE

> **"And he arose and came to his father. But when he was still a great way off, his father saw him and had compassion, and RAN and fell on his neck and kissed him.**
>
> **And the son said to him, 'Father, I have sinned against heaven and in your sight, and am no longer worthy to be called your son.'**
>
> **But the father said to his servants, 'Bring out the BEST robe and put it on him, and put a ring on his hand and sandals on his feet. And bring the fatted calf here and kill it, and let us eat and be merry; for this my son was dead and is alive again; he was lost and is found...'"**
>
> **(Luke 15:20-24)**

It's hard to read this story without getting teary-eyed. What a perfect picture of the nature of our Heavenly Father. I love the part that says the father "RAN" to greet his son. He didn't even wait for the son to get all the way to the house.

Notice that there was no lecture, no punishment, and thank God there was no condemnation. In fact, the father was so happy to have his son back home that he threw a party in celebration of his return!

Friend, perhaps you have wandered away from your Heavenly Father. Maybe your life is in shambles right now because of foolish decisions that you have made.

Maybe you have gotten yourself into such a financial bind that there doesn't appear to be any way out. My advice to you is, "COME BACK HOME!"

Your Heavenly Father will come running to meet you during your time of crisis. No matter what you have or haven't done, God still wants you to have money to survive, to provide for your family, and to keep your promises.

Chapter 6
Enjoying the Fruit of Your Labor

I trust that by now you are gaining a deeper understanding of the Divine purpose of wealth. There are at least seven reasons why God wants you to have money, and so far we have explored three of them. There is much more to come. Now, let's look at the fourth reason why God wants you to have money. Let's go to our most trusted source: The Holy Bible.

> **"and also that every man should eat and drink and ENJOY THE GOOD OF ALL HIS LABOR-it is the gift of God."**
> **(Ecclesiastes 3:13)**

The fourth reason why God wants you to have money is for you to *enjoy*. He not only wants you to have enough money to survive, enough to provide for your family, and enough to pay your debts; He also wants you to have plenty left over to *enjoy*.

What is the *"good of your labor"* that this verse mentions? The good of your labor is that little piece of paper that you get every Friday, every two weeks, or every month. It's called a paycheck.

The reason I know that this is the "good of your labor" is because if your boss told you that he wasn't going to pay you for a couple of weeks, and was going to give you the opportunity to work for him for free, I have a feeling you would take your labor somewhere else.

The "good of your labor" is simply the reward that you receive for your labor, which is the money you earn. God wants you to enjoy your paycheck. What is amazing to me is that I have yet to meet an unbeliever who questions this truth, but I have met multitudes of believers who struggle with accepting it.

Perhaps you recall the verse in Luke chapter sixteen that I mentioned, where Jesus said that the world exercises more wisdom than the Church does concerning practical matters like money. I am convinced that the primary reason for this is what I talked about in chapter five.

Those who struggle with accepting the fact that God wants them to have money to enjoy, simply do not understand the true nature of God, or their relationship with God. God is love, and love always gives. So the greatest manifestation of love is giving.

Now we believers know and readily accept that God gave His best gift, which is eternal life through Jesus Christ. But for some reason, many believers struggle with receiving material wealth.

I believe that this is a strategy of the enemy to confuse us about this vital subject. This is my purpose for writing this book. I have already stated that as you begin to better understand the Divine purpose of material wealth, it will be much more difficult for the enemy to talk you out of believing that God wants you to be wealthy.

If you can believe that God gave you His only begotten Son, it should be the easiest thing in the world for you to believe that God wants to give you material riches to enjoy. The following scriptures are so clear that you should never again question this fact:

> **"He who did not spare His own Son, but delivered Him up for us all, how shall He not with Him also freely give us ALL THINGS?"**
> **(Romans 8:32)**

> **"Charge them that are rich in this world, that they be not highminded, nor trust in uncertain riches, but in the living God, who giveth us richly ALL THINGS TO ENJOY."**
> **(1 Timothy 6:17, KJV)**

I don't see how the Lord could have made it any easier to understand. God wants you to have money so you can enjoy it. When God gave you Jesus, He also freely gave you ALL THINGS – not just "spiritual things" – ALL THINGS! All things would definitely include money.

I have already said more than once that money is the most common tool used to obtain all other things. So why has God freely given you ALL THINGS? He has given you all things for you to enjoy. Just in case you are still questioning this, here is another scripture for you straight from Jesus Himself:

> **"...Ask, and you will receive, THAT YOUR JOY MAY BE FULL."**
> **(John 16:24)**

Notice that your asking is not limited to "spiritual things." This verse plainly tells us that one source of joy in our lives is receiving what we ask for. When you ask for something, and receive it, doesn't it feel good? Doesn't it make you happy? God knew that in the beginning, before He ever created you. In fact, He's the One who made you that way.

God knew that, as physical beings in a physical Earth, we would receive pleasure and enjoyment from the rest of the "stuff" that He created. God knew that we would enjoy His STUFF. This is one of the reasons why He put the stuff here. He put it here for you to enjoy. So don't fall for the trick of the enemy. Stop feeling guilty about enjoying material wealth. Sinners don't feel guilty about it; why should you? If God put it here for anyone to enjoy, surely it would be for His children!

A Word Of Warning

The Bible does have a couple of words of caution along these lines. Here is the first one:

> "He who loves pleasure will be a poor man..."
> **(Proverbs 21:17)**

God made it clear that He wants you to have money to enjoy. We saw in Ecclesiastes that enjoying the reward of your labor is the *"gift of God."*

However, if you become a pleasure-lover, and you live your life only to go from one thrill to another, you'll eventually run out of things to thrill you, and you will definitely run out of money.

Even sin brings pleasure for a season, but does that mean that it's OK to sin? Of course not. Don't be like the prodigal son and spend ALL of your money on pleasure. Remember, there are at least six other reasons why God wants you to have money.

Another word of warning is found in the book of Deuteronomy:

> "When thou hast eaten and art full, then thou shalt bless the LORD thy God for the good land which he hath given thee. BEWARE THAT THOU FORGET NOT THE LORD THY GOD..."
> **(Deuteronomy 8:10-11, KJV)**

I have seen this happen many times. Someone will hit the bottom of life's barrel. They are completely broke, and their life is an absolute mess. Then, they turn to God. They begin to apply His principles, and the next thing you know their whole life turns around, including their finances.

Then, before long, they start missing a few church services. It seems harmless at first. Gradually they are missing the mid-week or evening service frequently. Then they begin to miss every once in a while on Sunday morning. Before long they are missing more than they are attending.

Eventually they just quit. They quit church and they quit on God. How could this possibly happen? It's easy. In fact, it could happen to anyone. They forgot where their blessings came from. They forgot the source. This is a picture of the nation of Israel over and over again in scripture.

Bondage...Repentance...Deliverance and Blessings Forgot the Lord...Back in Bondage

This is also a common pattern among believers today. This is why God made it a point to forewarn us. He knows that when prosperity comes, along with it comes the temptation to forget the true source. We must constantly stand guard over our lives to keep from giving in to this temptation.

More Than Enough
God wants you to have money to enjoy. There is no

question about it. I believe that one of the hindrances to the acceptance of this fact is the false belief that there is a shortage of natural resources on Earth.

If you believe that there is a limited supply of food, petroleum, gold, silver, and money, then you will probably feel guilty when you start to prosper. The enemy will come along and say, *"What right do you have to drive a nice car, live in a nice home, wear nice clothes, go on nice vacations, wear nice jewelry, and sport around on the lake in a nice boat, when millions of people don't even have enough food to eat?"*

He will remind you of all the starving children, and will try to convince you that it's your fault, because you are out spending your money having fun. Ask yourself this question: How much money can you give to help the starving children if you barely have enough to get by yourself? Don't you think that the person who has a surplus of money to enjoy is in a much better position to do something about the needs of others than the person who barely has enough to get by?

If there was a limited supply of resources, and my abundance caused someone else to lack, then I would be on the opposing side of the prosperity message. This is one of the most foolish notions I have ever heard. The only way I can ever do anything about someone else's lack is if I have *more* than enough.

First of all, let me assure you that there is no shortage of food or natural resources. The population explosion didn't come as a surprise to God. Do you think that

God, being the wise Master Planner, didn't consider how much it would take to sustain the human race until He returns? Can't you just picture the Lord saying to the angels, *"Whoops, I don't think I created enough gold! What are we going to do?"* I heard someone say once that there are more bananas that fall off of the trees and rot in the jungle, than are consumed by the rest of the people in the world. I haven't taken the time to research that, but in light of scripture it doesn't surprise me. Why? Because…

OUR GOD IS THE GOD WHO IS MORE THAN ENOUGH!

He has an unlimited supply! Your abundance does not create someone else's lack. There are many reasons for poverty and lack, but one thing is for sure, you enjoying the fruit of your labor is not one of those reasons. God wants you to have money to enjoy.

Chapter 7
Life's Greatest Blessing

So far we have discussed four significant reasons why God wants you to have money. I would like to introduce the fifth reason with a story.

I Don't Want To Be Rich
Many years ago I was in the real estate business. Every week, we toured the new properties that had been listed with our agency that week. Normally there were several of us in the group, but on this particular occasion it was just the two owners and me.

This man and his wife were also Christian people, so we had developed a good friendship. We often had discussions about the Bible, and this time we were discussing the subject of money. I will never forget that day as long as I live. The lady made a statement that I have heard many believers make. She said, *"I don't want to be rich. I just want enough to give the Lord His part, and to take care of my family."*

I didn't think much about what she said, and I didn't plan to comment on it. Then, all of a sudden, I heard these words coming out of my mouth. I said,

"WELL YOU'RE JUST STINGY, THAT'S WHAT YOU ARE!"

I was shocked! I couldn't believe my ears. Evidently my friends were shocked too. They both whirled around, and glared at me sitting in the back seat. Honest to goodness, the man was so startled by what I had said that he swerved the car on the road.

Still staring me right in the eye, the lady said, "Well, I want to know just what you mean by that." I was thinking, "So do I." I was just as surprised as they were.

Now keep in mind that this was all happening very quickly. But during those few seconds, I was already looking to the Lord for an answer. I was searching frantically for the words to answer her question. Thank God, after a short pause, the answer came.

I said, "That's the attitude of a lot of believers. They say they don't want to be rich. They think they are being humble, but they are really just being selfish. You said that you just wanted to give the Lord His ten percent, and have enough left over to take care of YOUR family, and nobody else."

I continued, "Who's going to send missionaries around the world? Who's going to build the Christian radio stations and television stations? Who's going to help get the Gospel to the ends of the Earth? If we Christians don't do it, it won't get done. And we can never do the job if we're just believing for enough for our own little family to get by. It's just selfish, that's all it is!"

She thought for a moment and said, "Well…I never thought of it like that before." I didn't say anything, but I was thinking, "Neither have I." The Spirit of God had just reinforced within me a belief that I had, but that I hadn't thought much about. What a revolutionary experience that was in my life.

One Word From God
I'm reminded of another similar story. This one happened on the night before my wedding. Back then, satellite services were popular in a lot of the independent churches. The congregation would come and watch national conventions and seminars on the big screen at church.

When we showed up at the church for our wedding rehearsal, there was a satellite seminar taking place, and Kenneth Copeland was teaching. He made a statement that I will never forget. Perhaps you have heard the phrase, *"Just one word from God can change your life forever."* Well, I can testify that this is true.

I can honestly say that this one statement by Brother Copeland radically changed by thinking concerning the prosperity message.

Remember I shared with you earlier that as a young guy I just wasn't interested in hearing about prosperity? Now that I look back, what better time could God have picked to help me change my views about money, than the night before I got married? Here's what Brother Copeland said. In his most authoritative voice, he shouted,

"IF ALL YOU NEED IS A DOLLAR A WEEK, BELIEVE GOD FOR A HUNDRED, AND GIVE THE OTHER NINETY NINE AWAY!"

Wow! Did you catch that? I can still hear Brother Copeland's voice in my mind, just as if it were yesterday. Something clicked inside of me. I got it! For the first time in my life I saw a true purpose for prosperity.

I had not yet lived long enough to understand that I would need money to survive, to provide for a family, and to pay debts. But now I realized that prosperity wasn't just for me. I saw just how ignorant and how selfish I had been. Now I understood. God wanted me to have more than enough money to take care of me, my family, and my debts.

God wanted me to have enough money to give some of it away. If you don't already have a firm grasp on this revelation, I pray that it is sinking in right now. God wants you to have money to give away. Let's find out who He wants you to give it to, and why.

"Let him who stole steal no longer, but rather let him labor, working with his

hands what is good, THAT HE MAY HAVE SOMETHING TO GIVE HIM WHO HAS NEED."
(Ephesians 4:28)

When I first saw this verse in the Bible, I was a little surprised. I remember asking my father-in-law after I had ministered on this verse in church, "Did you know that's why you were going to work tomorrow?"

He said, "No, I didn't." He was just as surprised as I was. It basically says that the reason you are going to that job every day is so you can have money to give to those in need. But what if someone has needs because of their own poor decisions? They probably do. We have already seen that bad decisions are one of the primary causes of financial lack.

So why would God expect you to take your hard-earned money, that you have invested several hours of your life to get, and give it to someone whose bad decisions have created needs in their life?

There are two reasons. First, this is God's nature. We have already talked about this. God is love, and the greatest manifestation of love is giving. God's love is also unconditional. He doesn't just give to those who deserve it, He gives freely to all those who will believe it and accept it. Thank God! Since God gives freely, He expects us to do the same.

"...Freely you have received, freely give."
(Matthew 10:8)

We have already seen that when God gave us Jesus, He also *"FREELY GAVE US ALL THINGS."* Now He says that because He has *given* to us unconditionally, He wants us to *give* unconditionally.

There is another reason why God wants you to have enough money to give some of it away. He wants you to get blessed!

> **"I have shown you in every way, by laboring like this, that you must support the weak. And remember the words of the Lord Jesus, that He said, 'It is more blessed to give than to receive.'"**
> **(Acts 20:35)**

Would you agree that receiving things you want is a great blessing? I enjoy receiving. There is nothing selfish about it. It is part of the nature of man, both believers and unbelievers alike. It's not only part of man's nature, but it is also part of God's nature. God enjoys receiving. But the Bible teaches that there is a greater blessing. What could possibly be better than receiving?

GIVING IS LIFE'S GREATEST BLESSING!

God wants you to give some of your money away to those in need, so you can enjoy the privilege of experiencing life's greatest blessing! Remember the words of Jesus that we looked at earlier,

> **"...ask, and ye shall receive, THAT YOUR JOY MAY BE FULL." (John 16:24, KJV)**

If asking and receiving brings such great joy, just imagine how full of joy you will be when you begin to give to those in need. This must be why God expects us to be *"CHEERFUL GIVERS."*

> **"So let each one give as he purposes in his heart, not grudgingly or of necessity; for God loves a CHEERFUL GIVER."**
> **(2 Corinthians 9:7)**

Not only will your joy be made full, but you will set in motion a process for your bank account to be made full as well. Just have a look at these next verses:

> **"He who has pity on the poor lends to the LORD, And HE WILL PAY BACK WHAT HE HAS GIVEN."**
> **(Proverbs 19:17)**

> **"He who gives to the poor WILL NOT LACK..."** **(Proverbs 28:27)**

Seedtime And Harvest
This law of giving and receiving is found in the first book of the Bible.

> **"While the earth remains, SEEDTIME AND HARVEST, Cold and heat, Winter and summer, And day and night Shall not cease."** **(Genesis 8:22)**

This principle of seedtime and harvest (giving and receiving) is repeated over and over throughout both the Old and the New Testament.

Here are a few New Testament verses:

> **"Give, and IT shall be given unto you; good measure, pressed down, and shaken together, and running over, shall men give into your bosom..."**
> **(Luke 6:38, KJV)**

> **"Be not deceived; God is not mocked: for WHATSOEVER a man soweth, that shall he also reap."**
> **(Galatians 6:7, KJV)**

I like the word "*IT*" and the word "*WHATSOEVER*" in these first two verses. This tells me that if I sow money through my giving, I am going to reap a harvest of money.

The money is going to come back to me, but it's going to come back with even more than I give. It's going to produce more, which is exactly what a seed is supposed to do. I also determine the size of my harvest through the size of my seed.

> **"But this I say: He who SOWS SPARINGLY will also REAP SPARINGLY, and he who SOWS BOUNTIFULLY will also REAP BOUNTIFULLY."**
> **(2 Corinthians 9:6)**

This is the principal of seedtime and harvest. God wants you to give money to those in need because He loves them, and because He wants you to prove His

LIFE'S GREATEST BLESSING

love to them through your giving. He also wants you to help meet the financial needs of others so you can experience the joy of giving. In addition, God wants you to give money to those in need, because the money takes on the nature of a seed, and it will produce a financial harvest in your life.

The Bible says a lot more about giving. I could teach on it for hours, possibly for days, or even weeks. The main thing I want you to see right now is that this is another one of the seven important reasons why God wants you to have money. God wants you to have money so you can give to those in need.

Chapter 8
Kingdom Building

I hope that you are enjoying reading this book as much as I am enjoying writing it. If so, then you should be getting pretty excited by now. We are on a journey through the Word of God discovering the *"Divine Purpose"* of material wealth.

Millions of people seek after and labor for money their entire lifetime, and never even understand why God wants them to have it. These same people will miss out on many of the blessings which money can provide. Aren't you glad that you're learning the true reasons why God wants you to have money?

The next reason why God wants you to have money still involves the principle of giving. We saw that God wants us to give to those in need. But that's not all.

I want to summarize this next type of giving as *"Kingdom Building."* God wants you to have money so you can give to help build His Kingdom.

"Hold on a minute. Do you mean to tell me that God needs my earthly riches to help build His Heavenly Kingdom?" Yes, that's right. God needs your money to build His Kingdom. Let's have a closer look.

The word "kingdom" is short for "king's domain." That's what a kingdom is. It is a king's domain. A kingdom is what a king rules over. It's more than just a piece of land or territory; it's the group of people who are subject to the king's rule. So God's Kingdom is the group of people who are under His rule.

This group of people is also known as His church, or His family. The Kingdom of God is the group of born-again believers who have received Jesus Christ as their Lord and their King. Hallelujah!

Working With God
God is building a Kingdom, and you and I are helping Him build it. Notice what the Spirit of God said through the Apostle Paul about *Kingdom Building*.

> **"For we are labourers together with God…"**
> **(1 Corinthians 3:9, KJV)**

Paul recognized that as a child of God, and as a minister, he was working with God. What was he working to accomplish? First, he was working with God to help get people into the Kingdom. The kings of the Earth have built kingdoms by conquering through war, slavery, and brute force. But we are helping God build His Kingdom through love. We are giving all people the opportunity to become a part of God's eternal Kingdom. So how do they get in? They become part of that Kingdom by hearing and believing the Gospel, which is the good news of eternal life through Jesus Christ. We aren't forcing people to join; we are giving them the opportunity to join.

"Brother Rich, I thought we were talking about money!" We are. I told you earlier that money has spiritual significance; now we are going to find out just how spiritual it really is. To become part of God's Kingdom, a person must hear the Gospel, believe it, and call upon the name of the Lord Jesus.

> **"For 'whoever CALLS on the name of the LORD shall be saved.' How then shall they call on Him in whom they have not believed? And how shall they BELIEVE in Him of whom they have not HEARD?..."**
> **(Romans 10:13-14)**

So before a person can believe, and call upon the name of Jesus, he must first HEAR the gospel. How is he going to hear? Let's look at the rest of this verse.

> **"...And how shall they hear without a PREACHER?"**
> **(Romans 10:14)**

In order for someone to hear the Gospel, a man, woman, or child must first preach the Gospel. Jesus doesn't preach the Gospel. Angels don't preach the Gospel. Only human beings can preach the Gospel.

Preaching the Gospel was part of the *"laboring together with God"* that Paul was talking about. In addition to preaching the Gospel to unbelievers, we are also called to make disciples, by teaching believers God's Kingdom principles. The following verses give us more insight into God's Kingdom-building plan.

> **"Go therefore and MAKE DISCIPLES of all the nations ... TEACHING THEM to observe all things that I have commanded you..." (Matthew 28:19-20)**

> **"And he gave some, apostles; and some, prophets; and some, evangelists; and some, pastors and teachers; FOR THE PERFECTING OF THE SAINTS, for the work of the ministry, for the edifying of the body of Christ." (Ephesians 4:11-12, KJV)**

Notice that our labor doesn't end when someone comes into the Kingdom. This is just the beginning. This verse says that God has set the ministry gifts in the church for the *"PERFECTING OF THE SAINTS."* So the second part of Kingdom building is ministering to believers. This is done by teaching the Word of God, so we can grow up in Christ and then reproduce ourselves in the world.

Here's where the money part comes in. Let's go back to the verse that we looked at a moment ago.

> "...And how shall they hear without a PREACHER?"
> **(Romans 10:14)**

Notice the second part of this verse:

> "...And how shall they preach unless they are SENT?"
> **(Romans 10:15)**

Think about this for a moment. How can the preacher or teacher be SENT without money? Notice it did not say *"how shall they preach unless they are CALLED?"* God CALLS people into the ministry, but we must SEND them with our financial support. This is the only way that a minister can possibly be sent.

Tithes and Offerings

This is not a new concept. It started thousands of years ago in Old Testament days. This is where the terms *"Tithes and Offerings"* took on their spiritual significance. An entire book could be written about the subject of tithing, but for now we will just introduce the concept, and the purpose behind it. The purpose for tithing was, and is, *Kingdom Building*.

In the Old Testament, there were twelve tribes of Israel. One tribe, called the Levites, was set apart as ministers. It was a tribe of priests. Their job was to minister to all the other tribes.

The ministry was their only occupation. They were not allowed to work another job or have a business on the side. In fact, they couldn't even own land. They were totally dependent on the other eleven tribes for their financial support.

The other eleven tribes were obligated, and commanded by God, to bring a *"tithe"* (ten percent of all of their increase) to support the Levites, so the Levites could in turn minister back to them the Word of God. It was a very simple but effective plan. Let's examine a few verses just to verify what I have told you.

> **"When the people of Israel give me a tenth of what they make, I will give that tenth to the Levites. This is their PAYMENT FOR THE WORK THEY DO serving at the Meeting Tent."**
> **(Numbers 18:21, NCV)**

> **"You may eat it in any place, you and your households, for it is your REWARD for your work in the tabernacle of meeting."**
> **(Numbers 18:31)**

> **"Moreover he commanded the people who dwelt in Jerusalem to contribute support for the priests and the Levites, that they might devote themselves to the Law of the LORD."**
> **(2 Chronicles 31:4)**

I'm amazed when I hear believers say that *"Tithing"* was just an Old Testament law. They reason that since we are no longer under "The Law" that tithing has been done away with.

I will certainly agree that tithing is no longer a law. It is much more than a law. Now tithing is something we do by faith, and not by force. As New Testament believers, we operate by a much higher law. It's called the *"Law of Love."*

The primary reason that someone would try to argue their way out of tithing is because they just don't have the faith to turn loose of the money, or they just don't understand why God introduced the system of tithing to begin with.

Tithing was made a law so the ministers, (the Levites) could build God's Kingdom, by ministering His Word to the people. If this is how *Kingdom Building* was financed in the Old Testament, by what other method can it be financed today? If God has come up with a new plan for providing for His New Testament ministers, I'm not aware of it.

The only way it is possible for God's ministers to build the Kingdom today is if the saints of God support them financially. If it took at least ten percent to get the job done back then, don't you think it would take at least ten percent today?

I mean, if we consider inflation, maybe we ought to just double it today!

Jesus and His Disciples

When Jesus called the original twelve disciples to work with Him in the ministry, do you realize that they all left their jobs and businesses to help build the Kingdom?

Peter was a fisherman, James and John left their fishing business, and Matthew quit his job as a tax collector. They all forsook their only means of income to go into the ministry with Jesus.

Have you ever thought about how the twelve provided for their families from that day forward? Think about it. Money had to come from somewhere. What about Jesus? It appears that Jesus worked with his earthly stepfather, Joseph, in the carpentry business up until the time that he entered the ministry.

How do you suppose that Jesus provided for his personal needs, and for his ministry employees? The Bible gives us the answer.

> **"After this, while Jesus was traveling through some cities and small towns, he preached and told the Good News about GOD'S KINGDOM. The twelve apostles were with him, and also some women who had been healed of sicknesses and evil spirits: Mary, called Magdalene, from whom seven demons had gone out; Joanna, the wife of Cuza (the manager of Herod's house); Susanna; and MANY OTHERS. THESE WOMEN USED**

> **THEIR OWN MONEY TO HELP JESUS AND HIS APOSTLES."**
> **(Luke 8:1-3, NCV)**

Even Jesus was dependent upon the financial support of the people to whom he ministered. Notice there were MANY who gave their money to help Jesus build God's Kingdom. The Apostle Paul makes more than one reference to the fact that God's system of financing the ministry still works the same way in the New Testament as it did in the Old Testament. Here's just one of those references.

> **"If we have sown SPIRITUAL THINGS for you, is it a great thing if we reap your MATERIAL THINGS?"**
> **(1 Corinthians 9:11)**

Before we bring this chapter to a close, I need to make sure you understand that God is a *GIVER,* not a *TAKER*. He doesn't want you to give ten percent of your money to the preacher so you and your family can go without. Here is a good verse that clearly illustrates the blessing associated with tithing:

> **"'Bring all the tithes into the storehouse, That there may be food in My house, And try Me now in this,' Says the LORD of hosts, 'If I will not open for you the windows of heaven And POUR OUT FOR YOU SUCH BLESSING That there will not be room enough to receive it.'"**
> **(Malachi 3:10)**

God dares us to put Him to the test in this verse. Just as we saw that there are multiplied blessings that come back to us when we give to those in need, the same is true with tithing and *Kingdom Building*. As we help build God's Kingdom, we get blessed!

Friend, the sixth reason why God wants you to have money is so you can set aside at least ten percent for God's ministers. God wants you to have money so you can help build His Kingdom.

Chapter 9
How Much Money Does God Want Me to Have?

God wants you to have money. So far we have discovered six reasons why. Let's have a quick review of these six reasons.

1. To Survive
2. To Provide For Your Family
3. To Pay Your Debts (Keep Your Promises)
4. To Enjoy
5. To Give To Those In Need
6. To Build The Kingdom Of God

Before I give you the seventh and final reason in this book, I want to answer a very important question. How much money does God want you to have? One thing we know for sure, if you don't have enough to cover the six things listed above, then you definitely don't have all that God wants you to have. Remember my real estate friend who said, *"I don't want to be rich"*? She was only wanting enough to survive, to take care of her family, and to give the Lord a little bit. That's great, but it's not enough to cover all of the Divine purposes of wealth outlined in the scriptures.

Super Abundance
"So Brother Rich, are you suggesting that God wants me to be rich?" Well, let's find out.

> **"And God is able to make all grace abound toward you, that you, ALWAYS having ALL SUFFICIENCY in ALL THINGS, may have an ABUNDANCE for EVERY GOOD WORK."**
> **(2 Corinthians 9:8)**

In my opinion, this is the most powerful prosperity verse in the entire Bible. Let's break this verse down word by word. I want you to really think about what is being said.

ALWAYS – Not one day of your life should you ever lack.

ALL SUFFICIENCY – You should always have enough money.

ALL THINGS – Enough to fulfill ALL of the Divine purposes of wealth

ABOUND – Be able to give A LOT of money

EVERY GOOD WORK – To every Kingdom-building ministry, and to every needy cause

Friend, this is a picture of SUPER ABUNDANCE! This is not someone who is just barely getting by. This is not someone who just tithes. This is an extremely wealthy person. This person is definitely able to survive. This person is able to provide abundantly for those in his house, parents in need, and any widows who are close relatives. This person has so much money that he is able to leave an inheritance that is more than his own children can spend. It is so much that it passes down to his grandchildren. This person never pays a bill or a debt even one day late.

The truth of the matter is that this individual probably does not have any debts, because they all have been paid. This person has plenty of money to enjoy. If they want to go anywhere in the world they just hop on a plane and go. They stay as long as they want to stay; they do anything they want to do; they buy anything they want to buy and they never have to worry about the cost.

They definitely don't read menus from right to left! They are not selfish. They are the opposite of selfish, because they have MORE THAN ENOUGH! They have enough money to give to those in need. Which people in need? They have enough money to help everyone they meet who has a need, even if the needs are huge. How do I know? The scripture says that they have *"AN ABUNDANCE"* to give to *"EVERY GOOD*

WORK." Not only do they have enough money to give to every needy cause, but they also have enough to give large sums of money to EVERY KINGDOM-BUILDING MINISTRY!

How many good works and needy causes are there in the world today? Just a few? No, you and I both know that there are many good ministries doing tremendous works for God. This scripture says that you should have enough money to give to every one of them. It not only says that you should have enough to give to every good work, it says that you should *"ABOUND"* (Give an abundance) to every good work. WOW! Are you getting the picture here?

If you've struggled with limiting views of prosperity, are those beliefs being challenged? I hope so. I hope that you are beginning to understand not only the importance of money, but also the importance of having an ABUNDANCE of money. So let me answer your question. Does God want you to be rich? YES! There is no way that we can draw any other conclusion from this verse in 2 Corinthians 9:8.

GOD WANTS YOU TO BE RICH!

Not just "spiritually" rich, but materially rich. God wants you to be a wealthy Christian. *"But Brother Rich, what if all that money were to cause me to backslide?"*

I have two things to say about that. First, thousands of people backslide every day who don't have much money. Money is not the cause of sin, it is simply a revealer of existing weaknesses. Notice the only person the Bible mentions who should worry about having too much money.

> **"...the prosperity of FOOLS shall destroy them."**
> **(Proverbs 1:32, KJV)**

Are you a fool? If you say *"No,"* then don't worry about money causing you to backslide. If you say *"Yes,"* then eventually your foolishness will destroy you, whether you have money or not. The answer for you is the wisdom of God, which comes from the Word of God. I have found that when I am really involved in giving to those in need, and to Kingdom-building ministries, I am much happier, much more fulfilled, and seem to walk much closer to God.

So, in my life, having more money helps me to become more spiritual, not less. I believe this is because when I get out from under the pressure of not having enough money, I can focus on the things of God more clearly, without being bombarded with thoughts of lack.

The Blessing Of The Lord
Have you noticed believers using this little phrase? They say, *"I got blessed"* or *"It was a blessing."* Look at what God says about His blessings:

> **"The blessing of the LORD, IT MAKETH RICH, and he addeth no sorrow with it."**
> **(Proverbs 10:22, KJV)**

One of the things that God's blessing will do is make you rich. *"Yes, but doesn't that just mean spiritually rich?"* Let's think about it. Can anyone who is not born again be *"spiritually"* rich? Of course not. They are separated from God, and therefore they are spiritually bankrupt. Do you realize that this verse is in the Old Testament, and was written to Old Testament believers who were not yet born again? Were they spiritually rich? I don't think so.

Also notice God said that sorrow would not come with these riches. If this verse were talking about becoming spiritually rich, then it wouldn't be necessary to say this. Obviously sorrow would not accompany spiritual riches. Many have become rich in this world, but they still are not happy or fulfilled. Why? Because they don't understand the Divine purposes for their riches, or for their life. Let's talk about this a little more. Does God's blessing really include making us rich?

> **"Now the LORD had said to Abram: 'Get out of your country, From your family And from your father's house, To a land that I will show you. I will make you a great nation; I WILL BLESS YOU And make your name great; And you shall be a blessing."**
>
> **(Genesis 12:1-2)**

God told Abraham, (then called Abram) "I'm going to bless you." So what did God's blessing include? We have seen that *"The blessing of the Lord maketh rich."* Does that mean financially rich? Well, let's see what happened to Abraham after he received... *"THE BLESSING OF THE LORD."*

> **"And Abram was VERY RICH IN CATTLE, IN SILVER, AND IN GOLD."**
> **(Genesis 13:2, KJV)**

I think we have our answer. God told Abraham, "I'm going to bless you." He kept His promise. He blessed Abraham, and as a result of that blessing Abraham became rich. Hundreds of years later, God reminded the children of Israel of this promise to Abraham:

> **"And you shall remember the LORD your God, for it is He who gives you power to get WEALTH, that He may establish His covenant which He swore to your fathers, as it is this day."**
> **(Deuteronomy 8:18)**

The New Century Version translation of this verse makes it a little easier to understand.

> **"but remember the Lord your God! It is he who gives you the power to become rich, keeping the agreement He promised to your ancestors..."**
> **(Deuteronomy 8:18, NCV)**

Who were the ancestors of the children of Israel to whom God made this promise of material wealth? One of them was their father, Abraham. God promised to bless Abraham, and that blessing included money.

Then hundreds of years later, God's blessing was still making His people rich. I have good news for you. God's blessing is still making His people rich today!

God wants you to have money. In fact, He wants you to have a lot of money, because it will require a lot of money for you to fulfill all of the Divine purposes of wealth in your life. We could say it like this:

"GOD WANTS YOU TO BE RICH!"

Perhaps you should pause for a few minutes and practice saying this to yourself right now. *"God wants me to be rich!"* Say it several times. *"GOD WANTS ME TO BE RICH!"* If you have trouble saying it, perhaps you still have some mental blocks because of wrong teaching, or because of being raised in a poor environment. I was raised on the other side of the tracks. Literally. We actually lived right by the railroad tracks, but we lived on the poor side. When I began to discover these truths about money in the Word of God, I made a decision that I would not let where I came from stop me from getting to where I wanted to go. It took a while to renew my mind to the fact that God wanted me to be wealthy, but thank God my beliefs eventually conformed to the Word of God.

Today I am reaping the rewards of the promise that God made to Abraham thousand of years ago, and restated in Proverbs 10:22...

"THE BLESSING OF THE LORD, IT MAKETH RICH…"

Chapter 10
The Father's Pleasure

Now we have come to the final chapter in our study of the *"Seven Reasons Why God Wants You To Have Money."* You've heard the saying, *"Save the best for last."* Perhaps this is what I've done, without even realizing it.

The first six reasons all have to do with human benefit. We saw how money affects you, your family, your creditors, those in need, ministers, and even the lost, who, through your giving, have an opportunity to hear the Gospel.

The next reason is a little different. I have already alluded to it several times. The seventh reason why God wants you to have money is for HIS benefit! "His benefit?" Yes. The first six reasons all have to do with man's benefit, but the seventh has to do with God's benefit. Let me explain.

Your Purpose In Life
To fully understand where I'm going with this thought, you must first understand the purpose for your creation and existence. I've heard many different teachings on this subject, and most of them were valid. However, I believe that all of the various reasons for man's creation and existence can be summarized in the following verse.

> **"Thou art worthy, O Lord, to receive glory and honour and power: for thou hast created all things, and FOR THY PLEASURE they are and were created."**
> **(Revelation 4:11, KJV)**

Have you ever questioned why you were created, or the meaning of your existence? Have you ever wondered, *"What is my purpose in life?"* Now you know. You were created for God's pleasure. God wanted you! Why?

Something about you has the potential to bring Him pleasure. God loves you unconditionally, and He has a great plan for your life. Included in that great plan is His great blessing, which we have clearly established includes material wealth.

> ***GOD WANTS YOU TO HAVE MONEY BECAUSE IT BRINGS HIM PLEASURE!***

Let's look at a couple of verses that verify this fact.

> "Let them shout for joy and be glad, Who favor my righteous cause; And let them say continually, Let the Lord be magnified, Who has PLEASURE IN THE PROSPERITY OF HIS SERVANT."
> (Psalm 35:27)

> "Beloved, I wish ABOVE ALL THINGS that thou mayest PROSPER and be in health, even as thy soul prospereth."
> (3 John 2, KJV)

If all things were created for God's pleasure, then money must have been created for His pleasure as well. God looked at everything He had created, and proclaimed, *"It is Good."* What is it about money that pleases God? He obviously doesn't need any of it in Heaven. Read a little about Heaven, and you will find that it is an extravagant place. So how could money possibly give God pleasure? I believe that I have found the answer.

> "Do not fear little flock, for it is your Father's GOOD PLEASURE TO GIVE YOU THE KINGDOM."
> (Luke 12:32)

> "...and to remember the words of the Lord Jesus, how he said, IT IS MORE BLESSED TO GIVE THAN TO RECEIVE."
> (Acts 20:35, KJV)

This is why God takes pleasure in your prosperity. This is why He has *"freely given you all things"* and why it is His *"good pleasure to give you the Kingdom."* God is love, and the greatest manifestation of love is giving. We have already seen that giving is life's greatest blessing. God is the Supreme Giver!

Not only has He given us all of the resources of the Earth, but He has also given us Heaven's best. He gave us Himself through His Son, Jesus.

Evidently, God finds His greatest pleasure in giving. This should not come as a surprise to us. If we can find pleasure in giving, then so must God, because we were created in His image and likeness.

Friend, God had plenty of money before He ever created man. But, evidently that wasn't enough to fulfill Him. God's "STUFF" was not enough to please Him, so He created us, just so He could have someone to whom He could give all the "STUFF."

God's greatest pleasure must come through giving to His children. Parents, this should be easy for you to understand. How do you feel when you are able to give stuff to your kids? The real joy of Christmas is the joy of giving. Oh yes, receiving is wonderful. But the greater joy, and the greater blessing is found in giving.

The only time that giving is not a blessing is when we are concerned about not having enough. I agree that this can limit our joy in giving. But what if you knew for sure that you had an unlimited supply of money?

The Father's Pleasure

How would you feel about giving then?

If you are a child of God, you have God's nature of love, so giving is part of your nature. Do you now see why God takes such pleasure in you having money? He knows that you need it to survive. He knows that you need it to provide for your family. He knows that you need it to keep your promises. He knows that you need it to enjoy life more fully. He knows the blessing that it will be to you to be able to help meet the needs of others, and He knows the necessity of money in building His Kingdom. These six reasons form the basis for number seven.

God wants you to have money because of the great pleasure that it brings to Him!

What if you went out next Christmas and bought your kids the very best that money could buy? I mean you gave them your very best.

Then everyone gathers around the Christmas tree and begins opening presents. One of your kids opens a present and says, *"How much do I owe you?* Or, *"What can I ever do to repay you?"* You would run for the phone to call a psychiatrist!

These are the people who try to buy God's blessings with their good works. They don't understand that IT'S CHRISTMAS TIME! The gifts are FREE! Then your next child opens his gift and says, *"I can't accept it. I've made too many mistakes this year. I've been more naughty than nice, and I'm just not worthy."*

You know who these people are. They have believed the enemy's lies, and have become victims of false doctrine. They have been led to believe that they just aren't worthy of God's blessings. They don't realize that IT'S CHRISTMAS TIME! God's gifts are FREE. He does not give to anyone based on worthiness. He gives because He loves us, and because He takes pleasure in giving. He gives because we are His children.

Then, another one of your children opens a very expensive gift and says, *"Oh my goodness, it's too much, it cost too much money. Don't you know that there are millions of babies starving in foreign countries? Please take it back. I can't accept it. It wouldn't be right for me to have it when millions of people don't even have enough to eat."* Another lie of the enemy.

Finally, one of your kids opens your gift, and just says, *"Thank you. It's just what I wanted. I love you!"* How would this make you feel? Nobody can ever convince me that it's not ...

"...MORE BLESSED TO GIVE THAN TO RECEIVE."

Words cannot begin to describe how it feels to bring that much joy to the life of another, especially your very own child. Imagine how God feels when we gladly receive all that He has given us. Don't let anyone or anything ever cause you to rob God of His greatest blessing, which is giving to you, His child. God wants you to have money because it brings Him great pleasure!

Closing Thoughts and Prayer

As I approached the completion of this book, this scripture began to stir inside of me:

"For what will it profit a man if he gains the whole world, and loses his own soul?"
(Mark 8:36)

Money is a great blessing, but it can never compare to a relationship with God through Jesus Christ. Material riches can last a lifetime, but at the end of your life… ETERNITY BEGINS. Eternity is a LONG TIME, and I know that you would rather spend it with God than separated from Him.

The Bible is very specific on what you must do to receive eternal life. I will give you a few scriptures, and then I'll lead you in a prayer. Here's what you must do to receive eternal life:

1. You MUST have a Savior.

Every human has sinned. *(Romans 3:23)*

Sin separates man from God, causes spiritual death, and creates the need for a Savior. *(Romans 6:23)*

Jesus is the ONLY WAY to God. *(John 14:6)*

Jesus is the ONLY WAY to be saved, and to receive eternal life. *(John 3:16, Acts 4:12, 1 John 5:11-13)*

2. You MUST Believe...

That Jesus is the Son of God. *(John 3:16, 1 John 4:15)*

That Jesus died on the cross to save you. *(John 3:16-17)*

That Jesus is the ONLY ONE who can save you, and give you eternal life. *(Acts 4:12, Acts 16:30-31, 1 John 5:11-13)*

That God raised Jesus from the dead, and JESUS IS ALIVE! *(Romans 10:9-10)*

That eternal life is a FREE GIFT. *(Ephesians 2:8-9, Romans 6:23, Romans 5:15-19)*

3. You MUST personally receive Jesus.

Everyone who receives Jesus becomes a child of God. *(John 1:12)*

Everyone who receives Jesus receives eternal life. *(1 John 5:11-13, Romans 6:23)*

Eternal life comes through knowing God, and knowing Jesus Christ (a personal relationship). *(John 17:3)*

How do I receive Jesus?
Everyone who calls upon the name of the Lord Jesus is saved and receives eternal life. *(Romans 10:13)*

Everyone who believes that God raised Jesus from the dead and confesses with their mouth that Jesus is their Lord, is saved and has eternal life. *(Romans 10:9-10)*

If you believe the scriptures that I've just shared with you, then you are ready to receive Jesus. It has nothing to do with how you feel, but rather with what you believe. We just read that you must CALL upon the name of Jesus, and CONFESS Him as your Lord. This is done through prayer (talking to God). I'll lead you in a simple prayer that you can pray out loud, right now, wherever you are. If you believe the words you are saying in the prayer, you will instantly receive Jesus Christ, be saved, and receive eternal life.

Your Prayer
"I believe that Jesus is the Son of God."

"I believe that He died on the cross to save me, and to give me eternal life.

"I believe that God raised Jesus from the dead, and He is alive.

"Jesus, I call upon your name.

"I receive you NOW as my Savior, and I confess that You are my Lord.

"I receive your FREE GIFT of eternal life.

"God, I believe that you are now my Father, I am your child, and I will spend eternity with You.

"Thank you."

Friend, if you prayed that prayer, please let us know. You have begun a new life in Christ here on Earth and you are assured of a place in Heaven for all eternity. Let us point you in the right direction and help you get started living for God, and growing up in Him.

Contact Information:
Rich Stocks Ministries
P.O. Box 701953
Tulsa, OK 74170

Phone: 1-888-275-5716
Email: info@richstocks.com

To order additional copies of this book, schedule meetings, or to find out about other teaching materials by Rich Stocks, please contact:

Rich Stocks Ministries
P.O. Box 701953
Tulsa, OK 74170

Phone: 1-888-275-5716
Email: info@richstocks.com